The Useless Bu

James Stamers

Alpha Editions

This edition published in 2024

ISBN : 9789362090836

Design and Setting By
Alpha Editions
www.alphaedis.com
Email - info@alphaedis.com

As per information held with us this book is in Public Domain. This book is a reproduction of an important historical work. Alpha Editions uses the best technology to reproduce historical work in the same manner it was first published to preserve its original nature. Any marks or number seen are left intentionally to preserve its true form.

THE USELESS BUGBREEDERS

THE USELESS BUGBREEDERS

BY JAMES STAMERS

TO THE SPACE COUNCIL, ASTEROID 4722 WAS JUST ANOTHER ROADBLOCK IN THE WAY OF INTERPLANETARY TRAFFIC. BUT TO THE USELESS BUGBREEDERS IT WAS HOME!

The previous case was a Weeper, and he lost. So the Space Zoning Commissioners were damp and irritable before I opened pleadings for my client. I tried not to squelch as I approached the bench.

"Not the Flammables again, Mr. Jones?" the fat Commissioner asked nastily, sponging his suit with a sodden handkerchief.

"This was last week, Your Honor."

The thin dark Commissioner stared pointedly at the charred end of the bench nearest the witness seat.

"Indeed it was, Mr. Jones."

The middle Commissioner poised his fingers and looked at the court ceiling; moisture gleamed diamond like on his bald head.

"Now let me see," he intoned. "Correct me if I err, Mr. Jones, but I seem to observe you have a habit of representing somewhat spectacular aliens. Including, in the past six months alone, the Drillers, Whirling Tombs, Fragile Glasses, Erupters, Vibrational Men, Transparent Women—and of course let us not forget the Flammables."

"I assure Your Honor, my present clients will be found to be sober, hardworking, desirable members of the Galactic Community, seeking only to live on their own asteroid in peace under a democratic system, which...."

"Thank you, Mr. Jones. Shall we proceed?"

"And perhaps," added the fat Commissioner, "you may be good enough to leave us with most of our courtroom intact on this occasion."

The thin Commissioner sighed and shuffled his papers.

"You appear, Mr. Jones, to contest a Space Council ruling for the elimination of Asteroid Four Thousand Seven Hundred and Twenty-Two on the grounds, which you allege, that it is a peaceful dwelling of an adult and responsible alien race."

"Yes, Your Honor."

"Then let us see your adult, um, Bugbreeder."

I shuffled uncomfortably and splashed the court stenographer who gave me a dirty look.

"A space tramp's name given in the early days of Space, Your Honor. More properly, my clients are the Selective Culturists of Bacteria and Lesser Life."

The fat Commissioner sniffed.

"Bugbreeders will do," he said. "Produce one."

My client hopped off the table and ran nimbly up to the witness seat. He sat there like a small green snowball with large and pointed ears.

"Happy, happy to be here, I'm sure," he said.

Fortunately he had a hand to raise and looked reasonably humanoid as he was sworn in. The caterpillar and semi-jelly cultures make a less favorable first impression, and at this point the Driller had gone excitedly through the floor.

"You are a representative member of your race?" I asked formally.

"Oh, yus. Much."

"And you reside on Asteroid Four Thousand Seven Hundred and Twenty-Two, the permanent dwelling of your race?"

"Oh, yus. Home."

"And although your home presents certain technical difficulties for interplanetary vehicles on the spacerun to the greater planets, you maintain it should be preserved because of your contribution to the culture of the Galactic Community?" I asked.

"Oh, yus."

"Does he understand a word you're saying, Mr. Jones?" asked the bald Commissioner.

"Oh, yus. Not much," said my client cheerfully.

"Hurrmph," I said, and coughed.

"Perhaps I may assist," suggested the thin Commissioner, with a nasty look at me. "What exactly does your race do?"

"Breed bugs, I'm sure. Am head bacteriophysicist name of Lood. Am good scientist."

"And what exactly do you do with these bugs you raise?"

"Most everything."

"Your Honors," I interrupted. "At this point I propose a few simple demonstrations of what Mr. Lood and his people can do."

"May I inquire if either of my learned brethren know any way in which we can charge Mr. Jones with rebuilding costs, if necessary?" asked the bald Commissioner.

"Your Honors, I assure you...."

"Proceed at your peril, Mr. Jones."

I walked over to the exhibit table and pointed to a row of jars.

"Exhibits A through G, Your Honors. Samples of food and beverages produced by my clients without raw materials and from the expert culture of bacteria."

I held up a jar full of mauve fungus. It was the most attractive example.

"I would hardly call feeding on funguses a sign of a responsible humanoid race, Mr. Jones."

"Perhaps Your Honor will recall the part played by bacteria in making milk, cheese, wine, beer, bread."

The Commissioners looked at each other and nodded reluctantly. So I passed the jars up to them, secure in the knowledge they had been tested by the Alien Foods Bureau. I watched the Commissioners unscrew the lids and taste the contents somewhat hesitantly.

"Not bad," confessed the fat Commissioner eventually.

"Quite palatable."

"Of course we already have honey and similar foodstuffs, Mr. Jones."

"Naturally, Your Honor. But Mr. Lood's race can survive without extraplanetary aid. Provided they have sunshine and water, they can breed their spores and bacteria with no other resources."

"You mean," said the thin Commissioner with a dark leer, "that almost any sunny planet would do for them?"

Somewhere along the line my point seemed to have been swept away, so I added hurriedly:

"I offer this evidence purely to show the high degree of civilization of my clients' culture, as cause why they should not be deprived of their native land."

"Oh, yus," my client agreed.

"Mr. Lood," intoned the bald Commissioner, "to stay on your present asteroid you will have to prove that your race offers something that cannot be found elsewhere in the Galactic Community. Now have these funguses of yours any special medicinal values, for example?"

"Please?"

"Can you cure diseases with them?"

"Oh, no."

"Ah," said the thin and fat Commissioners together. "Proceed, Mr. Jones."

That put Lood somewhere back behind the twentieth-century discoverers of penicillin and the myecins, and even back behind the pioneer Pasteur. Five hundred years back, in fact.

"Yes. Well. Let's see how my clients handle housing, Your Honors. I think you'll find this quite revolutionary. Mr. Lood?"

Lood hopped off the witness seat and trotted up to the long table normally reserved for attorneys. Lately, I have found my professional colleagues strangely reluctant to stay in court when I have a case, so Lood had the entire table to himself.

He pulled a small jar out from under the table and spread a pile of dust on the tabletop. Then he unscrewed the jar and gently poured nothing out of it onto the dust. Nothing visible, that is. But I assumed it was teeming with viruses and such.

"While Mr. Lood gets this started, Your Honors," I said, hoping the viruses or whatever were not fatal to humans, "may I submit the usefulness of fungus foods for space-travel and for pioneers on inhospitable planets?"

"Are we having difficulties with General Food-Concentrates, the Travelers Capsule Combine and the other ten thousand concerns in this line, Mr. Jones?" the bald Commissioner asked quietly.

You can't say I didn't try. I shut up and watched Lood fuss with the dust on the table.

It started moving as if it were bubbling and Lood stood back.

Slowly, the dust on the table formed itself into a brick, a long eight by six by three inch brick. Lood smiled happily.

"And here, Your Honors," I said triumphantly, "here is automatic housing."

"One brick does not make a house, Mr. Jones."

"If Your Honors will just watch...."

The brick slowly elongated and split into two perfect bricks, lying on the table end to end.

"Mass colony action of bacteria," said Lood wisely. "Oh, yus."

The two bricks each split into two further bricks. These divided and multiplied themselves while we watched, out to the end of the table.

"I would like Your Honors to observe the way these bricks overcome natural hazards," I said, getting into my stride.

I pointed to the bricks drooping over the end of the table. A brick fell onto the floor at each end, then built itself up until it joined the line of bricks on the table, forming a perfect arch at each angle. The line on the table was now three bricks high, so I walked round and stood behind the wall.

"You see, Your Honors, suppose I need a house. I merely combine these suitable microbes and dust. And there we are, a house."

I had to stand on tiptoe to finish the sentence because of the mathematics involved. Every brick was doubling and redoubling itself in just under a minute. And the wall was getting quite impressively high.

"Mr. Jones," called one of the Commissioners.

It was not until I tried to walk round the end of the wall that I found I had been out-flanked.

I ran to the nearest wall of the courtroom but the bricks got there first. I heard a rending noise that suggested the other end had gone clean through the opposite wall. As a matter of fact, I saw the astonished face of an attorney entering the main door of the Justice Building as the wall advanced towards him. Then he saw me. He grinned and waved.

I was in no mood to wave back.

"Mr. Lood, Mr. Lood," I yelled. "Can you hear me?"

"Wall too thick, yus," came a muffled answer.

And indeed it was. I had not noticed it, but the wall was expanding sideways as well. I was calculating the approximate thickness when it went up and through the roof of the courtroom.

Fortunately it was a nice sunny day.

However, this was no time to sunbathe and I dashed towards the hole in the courtroom wall, where Lood's wall had gone through.

I just got out before a buttress, coming out the wall at right angles, blocked the gap. I remembered something Lood had said about the automatic creation of full-scale houses on a simple standard plan: two rooms, a toilet and a patio.

Outside, the wall was well on the way towards completing its second simple house. This side of the wall was, that is. I could only assume it was doing something similar on the other side. There was no way of getting round and seeing, except by outstripping the wall in a sprint.

I gathered my breath and dignity and ran very rapidly down the length of the wall, round the far mounting tiers of brick, advancing now on the State Library, and back to where I had left the Commissioners and Mr. Lood.

I was faced by a thicket of patios and arched doorways and low-roofed houses.

"Your Honors, Your Honors," I called hopefully, walking into the maze, in the general direction of what appeared to be an old and ruined war monument. It then occurred to me that this was the outer wall of the courthouse. It stood far off, pointing a stone finger to the sky, as if going down in a sea of brick for the third time.

"Your Honors, Your Honors...."

I met them turning a corner.

Unfortunately, they seemed to have found it necessary to crawl through a broken gap of some sort. They were very dusty and had a slightly shredded appearance.

"Ah, Mr. Jones," they said grimly, dusting each other off.

A tremendous crash announced the falling in of the roof of the State Library.

"Well," said the thin Commissioner, "he did say it was revolutionary."

I smiled politely.

"Don't giggle, Mr. Jones, or we'll hold you in contempt."

We wound out of the maze in single file. A pattering behind us announced Lood bringing up the rear.

Once we were out, and about two hundred yards ahead of the advancing walls, patios and houses, the three Commissioners turned on me.

"Mr. Jones," they said with restraint. "You will now stop this reckless building project."

I turned to Lood.

"You must stop it," I said.

"Oh, yus," he agreed, nodding happily. "Most marvelous, no. Ample housing for all and sundry. Homes for peoples. Immediate occupancy. You like basic plan house, yus?"

"Mr. Lood," snarled the fat Commissioner. "The problem on every habitable planet so far has been to find room to build. Earth is congested...."

Distant crashing informed me that an unprecedented houseclearing was still going on.

"... And so are all authorized planets yet discovered. I speak for my learned brethren in saying that this ... this anthill of yours is one thing the Galactic Community can do without."

"And do without right now," added his bald colleague.

"You wish to stop?" asked Lood.

Small tears filled the periphery of his round eyes.

"Yes," I confirmed brutally. "Can you stop it?"

"Oh, yus. Must have antiseptics."

It took the fire department four hours of spraying from their copters to reduce the entire housing estate to dust. And then an even blanket of brown feathery residue lay unbroken for several acres, save here and there where the shells of previous buildings stood up gauntly and accusingly.

"All bugs gone," said Lood sadly.

"But what about this mess?" demanded the bald Commissioner.

"Comes out of air. Floating particles. Process cleans air, too."

A fresh wind from across the blanket of dust came inopportunely to punctuate Mr. Lood's remark. As soon as they could talk again, the Commissioners suggested resuming in another city.

"Assuming, Mr. Jones, you wish to produce further aspects of your, hum, case."

Six red and bleary eyes stared at me from a coating of brown dust of only vaguely judicial appearance.

"I think, Your Honors, the next evidence had better be delivered in the open," I said, and pointed to a nearby park.

Much, if not all, of the dust fell off us as we walked over to the small green hill in the center of the park. The birds twittered, the sun shone, the breeze was fresh; and after the Commissioners had settled on convenient tree stumps, I felt quite hopeful about the third line of evidence. Lood stood optimistically by.

"Your Honors," I said, "you are aware that Earth suffers a grave shortage of metals. Almost all economical quantities have been mined out. Yet, Your Honors—" I paused dramatically—"in the haematin of human blood alone, whose main function is to carry oxygen to the system, there is nearly twice as much iron by weight as oxygen."

"Precisely which of us, Mr. Jones, do you propose to mine first?"

I cleared my throat and let the thin Commissioner's remark pass.

"Merely making the point, Your Honor, that the metal-carrying properties of bacteria have been hardly considered."

This was stretching it a bit because selective breeding of microbes for the recovery of metals in tailings have been developed back in the nineteen-fifties. But so far as I knew, no one had carried it as far as my client race.

"Mr. Lood," I commanded.

"Just one moment, Mr. Jones," said the bald Commissioner drily. "Let us have an outline of this *before* we start."

"Certainly, Your Honor. Mr. Lood will now extract gold from a sample of ocean water we have obtained."

I signalled to the waiting carrier and it came trundling softly over the grass and deposited a large tank on the grass.

"Genuine untouched ocean water, Your Honors," I said, slapping the tank. "Go ahead, Mr. Lood."

The little fellow hopped up to the side of the tank and emptied another invisible horde from a test tube into the water.

We waited.

"Oh, yus," he said.

And there on the bottom of the tank was an unmistakable sludge of metallic gold, shining speckled in the rays of sunlight bending through the water.

I scooped out a sample and handed it round for the Commissioners to inspect.

"Subject to analysis," grunted the fat one, "this certainly seems to be gold."

"Of course, there is no reason why this should not be done on Earth, as a starting point."

The thin Commissioner paused and looked at my client.

"Does this process affect fish?"

"Oh, yus," said Lood. "Kills all parasites. Fish, reptiles, and such."

"Thank you," said the Commissioner drily.

Mr. Lood looked at me apologetically.

"My people too small to tolerate fish," he explained. "Fish most dangerous wild beasts. Oh, yus."

"Never mind," I reassured him. "Your Honors, I feel the court will take a more favorable view of the dry-land operation, then. Taking place as it does in the bowels of the earth, there is no danger to valuable livestock. And here we can demonstrate, for example, simple aluminum extraction, by the progressive reduction and oxidation and reduction of bacteria on a molecular scale.

"I hope," I added, "this experiment will produce visible evidence of this great boon to mankind, though I must ask Your Honors to watch closely."

Lood produced another test-tube, pressed a small hole in the grass with his finger and emptied the tube. The hole darkened.

We all bent over to watch.

Nothing happened.

"Perhaps a dud batch?" I asked eventually.

"Oh, no," said Lood.

We peered intently into the small hole without seeing anything.

Then a faint wisp of steam came out of the hole. I walked over the grass, picked up a long twig, walked back and thrust it into the hole. I could not touch bottom, so something was going on down there.

The edges of the hole began to gleam with white metal. I was about to explain the alumina content of common clay, when the thin Commissioner and the tree stump he was sitting on went down with a whistling sound into a sudden pit that opened beneath him.

I only just caught the third and last Commissioner in time. We watched his tree stump sinking out of sight together.

The ground began to quiver uneasily.

"Let us get out of here with all haste."

I followed the direction of the court with proper professional zeal. And we just made it to the safe stressed-concrete surface of the old freeway when the park melted completely into a stark framework of aluminum. Seated in the middle and peering at us through the aluminum cage were the other two Commissioners. They did not seem particularly happy.

Around them in a widening belt there opened up a pit of gleaming aluminum, melting, so to speak, towards the horizon on all sides.

"You realize, I suppose, Mr. Jones," said the bald Commissioner beside me, "that your client is in the process of eating up the Earth." He breathed heavily.

Lood was beaming and hopping up and down at the success of his experiment. I touched him in the general area of a shoulder. He looked at me.

"No," I said firmly, shaking my head.

"No?"

"No!"

His round eyes became tearful and his little green body shook.

"Oh, dear. Oh, dear. Oh, dear."

"Antiseptics?" I asked.

"Oh, yus," he confirmed sadly.

Very fortunately, the fire department was still observing my client—and me, I suspected afterwards, ridiculous as that may seem.

This time it took them several hours of deep spraying and drilling to confine the area. A vast saucer of aluminum remained.

"Useful for signalling to stars, oh, yus?" asked Lood, hopefully.

"Oh, no," I said.

A threatening cough made me turn round to see the three Commissioners staring at me.

"Mr. Jones...."

"... you have now destroyed the Courthouse, the Public Library and five city blocks...."

"... and buried them under a filthy layer of dust...."

"and reduced a park into a great garbage pit...."

"... we therefore refuse your claim and give you and your client six hours to get off Earth...."

"... and kindly do not trouble to advise us where the Space Council moves you. We will sleep more soundly for believing that it will be many, many light-years away."

And they turned and walked away, leaving me with my client—and, apparently, my traveling companion.

A quiet and suppressed sobbing made me turn and look at Lood. He wept dolefully.

"We have nothing," he said. "Oh, no. We have nothing to offer. Nothing that you humans want."

"Well," I said, "that's the way it goes sometimes."

And what, I wondered, was I going to do for a living now?

"Free food," gulped Lood. "Free housing. Free gold and metals. We had all hoped so much from this. Oh, yus."

There did not seem any point in telling him his people were several hundred years too late. Once upon a time he would have been hailed as a savior of a starving and poor human race, a great benefactor of mankind. Now he was just a nuisance. And I was another for letting him loose.

"Well," I assured him, "you have got one guest until they shift you off your asteroid. Me. Free food and housing will suit me fine. And maybe we'll find some very backward part of the Galaxy where they need gold and such.

"It's a pity," I added, as we started to walk towards the spaceport, "that you can't control these bacteria of yours."

"Can control."

"It didn't look like it, my friend."

"Oh, yus. Can control bodily leucocytes, corpuscles and such. Perfect cell replacement easy."

I looked down at him.

"If it's all that easy," I said. "I suppose your old men can run faster than your houses."

"No old men," said Lood.

"Well, old whatever-you-are's."

"No old. Not die. Oh, yus. Perfect cell replacement."

I stood very still.

"Do you mean you never die?" I asked.

"Oh, yus. Never die."

"Can teach?" I asked.

"Oh, yus. Most simple," smiled Lood. "Can teach all men not die. Not ever."

But I was off running after the three Commissioners, yelling until they stopped and stood waiting for me....